D1631912

n   o   p

q   r   s

t   u   v

w   x   y   z

The **First Skills** series includes seven books designed to help parents amuse, interest and at the same time teach their children. **Colours and shapes** and **abc** contribute to the child's early understanding of the reading process. **Counting** teaches him to recognize and understand simple numbers. **Telling the time** helps him to relate the time on a clock face to his everyday life and activities. **Big and little** deals with words that describe relative sizes and positions, all shown through objects and scenes that will be familiar to the young child. **Everyday words** helps him to enjoy and practise his vocabulary. **Verbs** will develop his early reading and language skills. In each book, bright, detailed, interesting illustrations combine with a simple and straightforward text to present fundamental concepts clearly and comprehensibly.

As you read together, practise saying the letter sounds. Remember that the letter name is **A**, as in ABC and the sound is **a** as in apple. Help your child to trace the letter with his finger and to write it in the air. Singing the alphabet and the letter names is a great way to remember the sequence. Making letter shapes using play dough will help, too.

A catalogue record for this book is available form the British Library

Published by Ladybird Books Ltd
80 Strand London WC2R 0RL
A Penguin Company

2 4 6 8 10 9 7 5 3
© LADYBIRD BOOKS LTD MMVI

LADYBIRD and the device of a Ladybird are trademarks of Ladybird Books Ltd

Printed in Italy

abc

by Lesley Clark
photography by Garie Hind

a

apple

alligator

ambulance

astronaut

b

baby

ball

banana

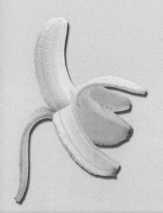

bus

C

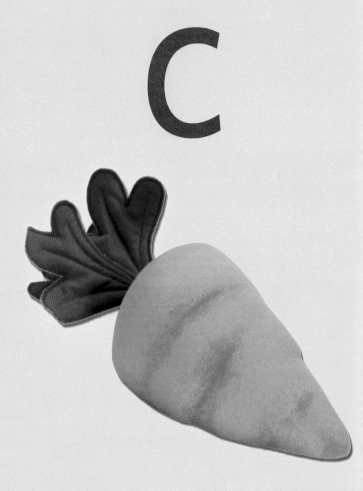

carrot

car

cat

comb

d

doll

dinosaur

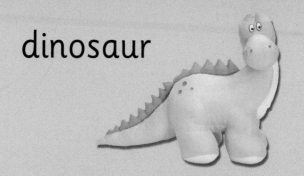

dog

duck

e

egg

elephant

envelope

exit

exit

f

fish

fan

fork

feather

g

girl

gate

 goat

guitar

h

house

hat

helicopter

horse

i

You're Invited
to a Party

at _____

_____

date _____

time _____

from _____

R.S.V.P.

invitation

j

jigsaw

k

king

kangaroo

keys

kite

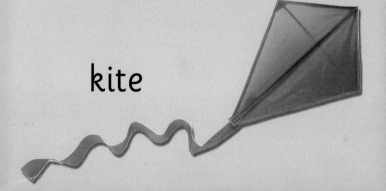

l

lion

ladybird

lamb

leaf

m

mug

monkey

mouse

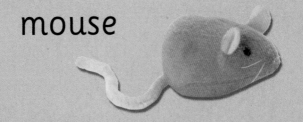

motorbike

n

nurse

O

orange

painting

pencil

penguin

pineapple

q

queen

r

rocket

S

socks

sandwich

shorts

soap

t

telephone

tiger

tortoise

toothbrush

u

umbrella

underwear

up

upside
down

V

vet

van

vase

video cassette

watch

X

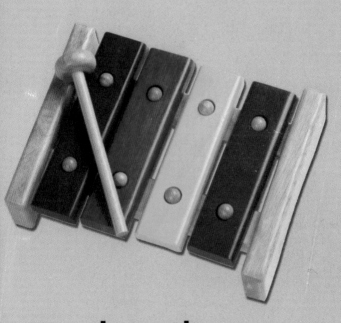

xylophone

y

yo-yo